Thoughts Along The Way

Contents

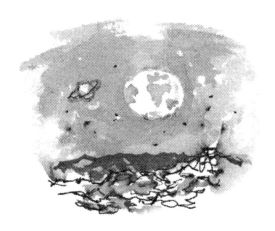

A Progress

Before the beginning God's light pervaded
the mystery of mists and vapours,
travelled through the realms of space
and dwelt between the tiny, unimaginable atoms.
His design brought form and structure to the universe
and was the beauty and the goodness
in the disordered evolution of mankind's being.

At a point in time, or gradual blur of centuries,
living creatures entered into His own image
and along the path received His gift of soul.
Whether from his early start
mankind possessed both mind and heart
or from the Earth's great distillation
did these grow on from contemplation?
We only know the rabid dawn of global mass
was mellowed down for man to pass.

What stage of gentle evolution
brought sufficient richness to our minds
to make us men? Our bodies strong and balanced –
a million years of growth and evolution –
yet what brought our minds to equal that fertility
and what became the start of man's humanity?

Was it the quest of our own origin that turned
   the key?
Did we search and ask and think
and then assume a god beyond the brink?
Were these our early stepping stones to wisdom,
the beginning of the human psyche
and was our soul implanted then
and was this the time we became real men?

Along that wavering line of evolution,
that ebbs and flows before it floods,
Did some begin as men with living souls
when others, from the same sired loins,
received just life and truly died.

It was not speech that marked the moment,
as other creatures transfer their thoughts by sound,
enjoy emotions and have their earthly fears,
but still no souls.

Is this the nub:
that the knowledge of a promised life beyond this
    world
makes us different from all other creatures,
those living packs that truly die?
But why to us this gift
that was not earned but absolutely given?

Were certain clans of these new men
made for God's companionship
and blessed by Him as chosen people?
Are they the first or, maybe even still,
the only tribe eligible for heaven?

The scheme of stars and suns and satellitic moons
hurled out in space and open distance,
cuts down our solar scale to grains of brief existence.
So vast at first – our little world declines
as realization sweeps our minds
and places us remoter still,
from all His love and care and skill.

Yet we are close and from our birth
are the stewards of this Universe
diminutive in space and time
yet powerful with our grasp divine.

Beyond our constellations seen from earth,
and to the edge of known space,
Does it all repeat again and are there other Betelgeuse,
Orions and a second Plough?
Each star a sun and in their firmaments more earths,
once in the past or in the future still to come,
the home of creatures, made like us and God's
    evangelical son?

Or do our souls inhabit them?
Are we a community of men
propelled, in negative time, from realm to realm and
    living heavens?
I do not doubt a detailed plan, but His endorsement
    would enshrine
the certainty for all mankind.

But was not our fragment of it all – our earth
the chosen place for the Mangod's birth?
Surely this great confirmation is sufficient
    explanation,
we need not doubt or search the more
we've been taught existence core.

But the limitation to one planet, since time began
ten billion men upon its rim,
makes crowded heaven a daunting place
for all of us who seek His face.

Would not more likely be that human man's
    intelligence and soul
on death, departed unto another world,
but not in light years but at timeless speed;
just as He transcends to meet our need.

Such gift to us would show more love
to top that which we have been given here,
and timelessness, with intelligence to know,
would fill our cup to overflow.
Do thoughts, as these, outrun our need,
for earthly miracles astound our little understanding
and reveal, to those who seek, the triumph of the
    planning.

Although the fringe of knowledge and a fragment,
    just,
of wisdom have we found,
the void, unknown to us still, is vast
will death's kind hand reward with anything we ask?

Is it a sin to speculate on that, which, if I love, then
    I will share
with Him – when He is ready?
Born with willpower and with love to make some
    choices mine,
for me, to speculate is but to reach and search
and surely seeking is our right divine.

That atheistic, agnostic breed of men,
who calculate the path of time
and prove, with God's own numeracy, His non
    existence
and all His gifts consign to evolution;
they delve beginning, but never see the start,
that spark or pre-spark of God's eternalism.

Man did take man's life on circumstantial evidence
and claim that evidence, so great, was good as proof
and therefore equal to the capital punishment that
    they could give.
If this was good enough for that then, surely,
    all around is good enough for proof?

Is the essence of all our seeking the structured use
    of time?
Have we followed logical steps and climbed a path
each day to mark a further step in life's progression
and onwards to perpetual life divine?

Or is time a concept just to quiet
our simple minds and justify our ageing bodies?
It cannot be a final definition,
that's still a path to search and find.

If time is as we think it
then what exclusive share of His attention could
    we receive?
Five billion living now and the same before us
and before the end how many billion more?
In terms of time what are five billion seconds
if just a second were the most we could enjoy?
If this, my hypothetical question,
is used to test a simple supposition
then we must wait two mortal lifetimes of our kin
before our turn arrives to be alone with Him.

So time must be a human inspiration,
of man's too logical imagination,
that leads us on to inevitably discover
that all our brains and minds are cover,
still too puny, all too small,
to grasp the explanation of it all.

Our chance to be alone with Him
lies in our understanding.
The whole of life can be with Him.
It is our choice to understand
and so discover what's in our hand.
For He is in our being, the origin of our thought,
that stays inside until we outside report.
We have a life time with Him to speak
but need to learn and first be meek.

For us new men, who on this earth have recently
    arrived,
He designed this rim for us to build our hives,
and although He tells us, our outward body is, like
    His too
it is our hearts and minds that we mould
    along the journey through,
This is lifes purpose, there can be no other,
this is the core of reason for every sister-brother.

The battle of my mind and gentle fear was once
the giving up of me and brain and individuality,
when loving death arrives to take me on.
The time and distance are a thrill
but loss of me a bitter pill,
that I should disappear, all personality absorbed
became the test I once mechanically abhorred.
But now I readily accept
to be a living fragment of His concept.

Original Thought

Where did my thought come from?
From within my body, mind or from my soul?
Was it always there and I just uncovered
or was it created in the moment I discovered
its picture on my living screen
that, by unspoken words and newly seen,
it formed a concept.

So where do my thoughts originate,
do I search and strive and contemplate
and write and string
successive concepts till they wing,
each well known until the last, sublime,
becomes a form of mystery that is mine,
all thoughts before empirically known
but, this the last, from within me, originally
    grown.

Then from whence the first:
was it carried from my birth
but I knew not then, as I now know,
my mind, like body had to grow?
So, when my first original thought
identifying me from what I'd been taught,
that constructive moment of my being;
some written down in words, some singing.
All created from that store of sound
that for all Gods earthly men abounds,
open to all eternity, yet there'd been no other
who knew the words that I would utter.

Only I can have my thoughts
and from them identify my being,
learn from them what kind of man
inhabits this body for my span
of time on earth, but do I know
what deeper thoughts within me flow?
As yet untapped, unformed material
needing to become an endless serial
of worthwhile revelations
on which to base my life's foundations.

My little thoughts, comments, revisions
all stem at first from chance collisions,
these are the test of my imagination
and mark the start of concentration,
from spark to flame and then to fuller fire,
in rapid growth until I tire
and turn away, until some day
I try again to delve the mystery of my brain
and follow down that path again.

I know this now: the more I think
and search and reach out to the brink,
as deep as I can delve and grow
the mystery and the route I go
are intrepid journeys for my soul to travel
but all lead me to a tabernacle.
As my living mind leaves my cradle earth,
the foundation rock that held my birth,
I soar in distant space and open time,
and enjoy the loneliness that is mine.
And I continue, when I can
and nearly find an earthly plan.

Have I a right to journey thus?
A given freedom – not trespass,
all through this vast, this great creation
I feel guided, drawn and on rare occasion
think – a glimpse of Him I see,
above it all in majesty.
As He, the owner, maker, builder
makes my life serene and fuller
I, of course, now know
where comes the thought, the source, the flow.
He is my maker, my originator,
by whom, with love, my thought was planted,
O how great the search in me He started.

*   *   *

My God within
with all my sin
are oil and water
yet all contained
in this my soul
I try to alter.

A cacophony of senses,
of love and folly
some genuine, some false pretenses.
The mix is me
from what life condenses.

Unification

Are our differences the simple depth of prayer
or is it warmth and sterner love?
Are the greater disciplines to life
a tighter freedom that gives us more,
a trodden path with deeper steps,
a narrower one made straight by search?

Yet add this century's changes to our lives,
the electronic newness of this living generation,
the teeming tribes and mixed-up races,
more millions live in clever places,
new sciences and greater comprehension
that's moved so much beyond contention.

All this has forced a massive change,
unknown and unrealized yet,
mankind is set upon a quest
of materialistic fantasy, a survival test
in competitive pressure and hurried preservation.
No time for thoughts of love or hope
to ease the growing consternation.

The modern churches, in all humility, do strive
to adapt and change to stay alive,
but liberalism erodes their rock,
that mankind needs to help him stop
his headlong flight to self-destruction.

The rock in Rome, is Christianity's foundation,
its truth and faith are mankind's consolation,
rigid to change but not from changes fears,
as, problems grasped, it comprehends the living mad
and sees their shame, their destitution.
It beams God's light on mans' confusion
and says what's bad, what's deeply wrong
repeats old prayers, unpopular and strong.

Until, at last, all men must recognize old patterns
follow again the ways that lead to hope and promise
and learn the peace that leads to love
and follow the patterns made for man by God.
How long this process, how long is time?
Depends it not on churches, hearts and minds.
This race of men are moving slowly
their survival needs one Church all holy.

O Lord who came for man to crucify
grant us now one church to unify
and fulfil ecumenical desires,
now lost in shrines and towers and spires.
The bible is the font for all of us
let us all be one in the church of Jesus.

Independence

Man's independence should be in all things but his
    spirit,
for rugged life demands all his strength and will;
born into him from women's greater instinct,
for she knows the space in life that he must fill.
The crowded lives of ever constant striving
demanding frame and brain to be in all supreme,
a mind incisive to every bold decision
and shoulders broad enough to drive a team.

But independence stems from successful competition
yet absent love, but also measures strength
and has resulted in man's physical condition
and produced a man adapted for this length.
Despite our lurches into foreign wars and famine,
both instruments of progress in their way,
the specimen that's here in God's own likeness
could be seen to be the one that's here to stay:
scientifically progressive and all seeking,
supporting greater numbers on this rim,
striving hard to beat his hungry, weaker neighbour
and taking full advantage over him.

This specimen, that's grown here from Eden,
passing by the Cross with only glance and shrug,
surely now must learn eternity's last lesson
and know he must convert to faith and love.
He needs to know the universe's reasons
and grasp its truth if he's a breed to stay,
the world is running out from constant taking
of things that man has never thought to pay.

For centuries, even longer, throughout all ages,
God's signs to man have been both subtle and
    unseen,
they've needed faith and deepest concentration
to make the frightened man turn from his dream.
Not wanting a difficult interpretation,
his daily lot has taken all his time
and greed has been his constant, lifetime's master,
so he's turned away and never seen a sign.

Although God's signs have been forever present
it's needed those who understood to show the way.
Noah's saving expedition was his fulfilment,
the rainbow in the sky the sign to-day.
The chosen people had quail and fallen manna,
as food to eat but also as a sign,
led by Moses, with the ark always beside him
and prophets all along the route down time.
They had very special heavenly attention,
then holocaust to make us see the sign,
it led on, for them, to land and home and freedom
and left the world to ponder on the crime.

How many are Our Lady's known visits,
and scores unknown, yet seen by someone every day?
The spinning sun, unknown but for those who see it
and for them alone, upon the day they pray.
Those secret things that only we can know about
and know that no one else can know them too,
these are the special signs of glory made for each of us,
as only we can know the moment they come true.

Are not these signs and messages to learn from,
to grasp, if man is on this earth to stay
but why so difficult and remotely distant,
so hard to learn or see along the way?
Cannot a message be loud and instantly be visible,
for those whose feet, like ours, are in the clay.
Why be hidden in the eyes of starving children
or broken bodies on a burning bier,
in tragic sights in life's revolving cycle
in death and wars and pain and human fear.
Why does God seem to speak to us through others
and not tell in simple terms what we're to do.
Why hang upon a cross to save humanity
when so few were ever there to see it through.

Is that then why we are so independent,
standing alone, 'gainst heaven, God and man,
confused and dazed awaiting confirmation
that God exists and even has a plan.
Our Maker's greatest sign, for some is still
contentious,
that Jesus came as God into our world,
His message, so different from all others
is in all men's hearts but lies there tightly furled:
to love our hurtful, spiteful neighbour seems
unnatural,
yet only love will break the evil spell
and let man bloom into human greatness
and turn the world to paradise from hell.

15

Is it because we've grown so hard and very complex
and only in our heart He wants his words,
our mind and muscles ours, but just for living,
our heart and spirit His to write his words?
Man's independence and his self-imagined greatness
are a mix resulting from his growth and strife
but soon he'll spoil this world of his for ever
and strip it bare and take away its life.

So he must find the signs of love that are all round
    him,
and give up that independence in his bones,
realize we do not mould our minds, control our
    movements
and nothing that we deeply love is all our own.

Let's learn to find the God that is within us,
the God of tender hearts and subtle signs.
Let's grasp the message that is planted in us
and turn our hearts and independent minds
to truth, with love and full dependence on Him
and find that ancient love, within us all, that binds.

World Pollution

We have trod the worldly path as man
but torn the fabric of the plan.
We've marred the earth, the air and water,
created nothing – only alter.
Sons learn not from experienced fathers,
each generation repeats disaster.
The mind of man has not developed
his human instincts remain enveloped
in locked-in passions, all impure,
and as a species cannot endure.

How can man learn to grasp God's meaning,
love the ailing world that's teeming,
protect old art while modern sciences searching,
respect old plans yet move on further
retaining all the old men's fervour,
explore worn trails, lost routes and broken casts
and from all this remould his life from what is past.

Those chippings from the dome of golden knowledge
have made our history and borne a faith for man,
they knead a bread of deeper understanding
to be the food for life's eternal span.
Patience and constant search reveal those chippings
and love and trust do fire the stove for baking,
let's work together for a great renaissance
and restore old Eden for our God again.

Realization

For months and years I waited for a shaft of light
to make the parables of my thoughts glow bright –
so that over me, all I'd been taught
could break, until some latent thought
would shine and lovingly divine
the depths of this my puny mind.

This crowded life is contradiction,
tragedy, hate yet benediction.
Of grace I've learnt and read God's Word,
an inner call I've sometimes heard,
have faith and look for resurrection,
always fearful of rejection.

My study and my meditation
encouraged deeper dedication
but, then I saw outside my cell
how fellow man and women dwell,
I knew their life: their competition,
abortion, war, their life's perdition.

The church for the modern life of man
is separate now, it does not span
the pious hopes of days gone by,
nor draw us in, inspired to try.
How can we meet those old endeavours?
With a divided church our lives are embers.

What is the balance that will hold us straight
should we learn to love and mediate?
Is it not now for us to seek the way
and map the course to follow every day?

We make up the church – we provide the balance
He gave us all our special talents.

Clichés and Rhymes

Twice now I've not known the number:
the one you don't know when you're very rich
and the one when you are not.

It's strange how monotonous it is
its round and round and up and down
at least when one is young or very young
For me it's only words that slip my tongue.

I once had ironed it out, or nearly so,
but it was wrong to solve it all, just pass it on,
and take away the joy and stress,
no need to plough, no fuss, no mess,
as stormless life leads to life's decay
and none I love I want that way.

It was when they said it's 'not for us'
but fought on still for 'theirs'
I felt the stir, that I'd once known,
and knew they loved their heirs.

*　　*　　*

I thought you'd phoned but 'twas not you,
another moved my mind away
from hope and every happy day.
But as I sit and hunger still
I wonder whether you will fill
my tireless days.
I know you will.

Patience

The heat of life it beat me down
yet I absorbed its rays
and turned them into tireless ways
of living in that sun.

But now should I abandon this rich heat
and go in shadow to some retreat,
be – 'driven out', – 'gone away'
why should I want this life to stay?

The little burn, not meant for you,
is from the heat, so freely given,
it is the daily heat of heaven
sent to remind us, as a token,
of the Word that God has spoken
It is that man and sun
will all – one day be one

*　　*　　*

The content, rhythm and the rhyme
are thoughts and music that are mine
the words that flood
come from my blood
that heals and cools with love and time.

*　　*　　*

With Apologies

If all good theologians are on heaven bent
then where go those to whom that this gift
    was never sent?
Are they to struggle in the mire of fate
and never see the Lord benignant?
But intellectual learning and description
are not enough to steal all benediction,
as all are welcome to the heavenly feast
the simple, great, and even our own parish
    priest.

The Power

O God are you the care
that drifts the parachuted pollen
to its chosen growing place?

Are you the force
inside the laden, druggèd, worker bee
that fills the honey cells abrim?

The charge that fuses
torpid, summer skies to burst
with golden edges into descending rain?

The gentle winter mist
and layered snow, that lines the valleys,
preserving still the summer warmth?

Are you the God who fills the tiny part
    I play with life,
firing my living energy with light?
I know you are.

The Seed

Why bother to grow a root
when all above is bright and wide?
Why tunnel deep, as if to hide,
When all is safe and warm outside and,
like a flute, life calls enchantment?

Does the earth hold such treasures
that I must grow my roots in it?
I know not, but my instinct says of course
    my roots
will hold my head up and, if I had no roots,
I'd never hear those gentle flutes.

On My Wife's Birthday

I wish to make a speech – so much to say,
because it's to my love, upon her Day.
A day so shunned before
it was, – 'O! such a bore'.
To have a birthday adding one more year
to life, its joy, its tiny fear.

O I hope I speak and true,
for I love you as I do
but now I only want to say
Here's to another day,
    another day,
        another day.

Some Beautiful Evidence

The jade of southern Asian hills,
bright children astride dark buffaloes,
tumbling badger kits in native daffodils,
all born new together.

The fury of black clouds pierced by golden light,
woolly mists in early morn enfolding villages still warm.
The rippled sea and just beneath the glorious colours of
    the reef.
The sun on patchwork crops of brown and green
From up high on hills and mountains seen.
A baby's smile, sweet, warm affection
A man and woman's love – perfection.

These surely show to man God's glory
His mystery, might, our living story,
perfectly conceived and planned,
the caring work of one great hand.
How could mere chance and time
create such life and world sublime?

Conversion

To grow from class to class and savour all the thrill
  of growing,
of moving up those flattering scales and knowing
that it was I who made the notes and knew it,
that it was from my aim and striving,
the reason for my life and driving
that made it come about – for I was strong.

But then I found the greater strength of wisdom
and lost my aim and found a new warm Christendom.
I wallowed for a time in chilling warmth,
some days were full but others nought
and then I professed a search and thought I knew –
I would just live it through,
be a hermit on a hill or in a hut,
escape and quit my earthly rut,
fast and pray and be alone
but, then I learnt – it's simply life I must condone.

Ultimate Warmth

I pray for God's warm sun to mellow my cold
  mind
As, in my busy daily life,
it reflects it back, not fills me warm,
I hanker to be heated through.

In Gozo's clime
I sat, beneath a fig, to pray away a day
but then returned to London's strife
to days of work, my daunting life.

But now, it's that I may fly away again,
beyond the Med to proper heat, though 'tis
    winter there,
beyond the middle line
and to its drought and heat and dust,
its sweat and work and men and lust:
to frightening numbers cruel and bleak,
yet still a moment in the loving sun I'll seek.

The sun is God's repeated sign to man
I hope to follow when,
my dutiful and marvellous span
is finished here and all my loving work is done
and I can rise and follow then, the sun.

No Further

The single Church, ordained by Christ,
was straight and simple to behold
but with his frail, though best intentions,
man tampered with that sacred mould
and let the freedom of his mind
evolve a church of a different kind.

We excused denominations
as adaptations for changing nations,
submitted to rulers' reformations
and lived through gradual transformations.

But in the end an Archbishop of our land
said publicly that our church must keep up with
   'the times'
and in a phrase he lost our Church,
our rock, our strength and almost our salvation.

The times are not the will of God
our times are what we've made them
and surely we must change our ways
but not His Church.

Recollections

Do you know those places,
where the gentle seas slide
cross sparkling sand and
the salt smell and bright sun
lift the heart and then
steal back and chill the toes.

Did you know those timeless places
that made up childhood's joy and
lasted the span of lifetime's memory?
Were those moments made
for childhood fun or grown man's security
that, delving memory, he would find himself again.

*   *   *

My Favourites

Do the smells of wood smoke,
the tug of wild fish,
early season mist,
cobwebs dew dusted,
high summer in a scented garden,
a solo nightingale,
the crunch of snow and crisp of leaves,
a dolphin leap,
the taste of carrot plucked from earth,
the needle teeth of puppy dogs and babies' nails,
the smell of incense and prayer,
Beethoven by the fire in winter
and children's laughter
stir your heart as they do mine?

Returning From Moscow

It's seeing it again, after such a pause in time
from a cold and foreign clime
that makes me know how soft my England is.
Even high above, at twenty thousand feet it's safe
and down on earth, at human levels seen,
it's warm and grey and sometimes green.

It is the best of all God's world
and although my life upon its rim
is centuries late to satisfy my whim,
I am grateful to exist at all
and from this home await my call.

A Little Thought

Is there a reason why intellect and mental
    concentration
is so oft enshelled in physical degeneration?
Are face and loveliness so shunned
that original thought aspires
only from bodies old and tired?

It is a fact that men and womankind
have in the past been quite blind
as, in growing numbers, they spend their time
at first, to enhance their given faces
and then work their bodies out for graces,
at last, when beauty has escaped them,
turn frustratedly to contemplation.

Surely brain and beauty could together
occupy this shell of ours
and exist beside our living soul
and from this great and lovely combination
spawn new dreams and thoughts about creation.

A Conversation Between Good and Evil

(An Extract from the Script of the Wintershall Nativity Play)

Herod   I seek the child, kill all the children.
Destroy this challenge to my power,
I brought the Jews to Nationhood,
I am the King where no one stood.

Destroy this challenge to my reign
tread it out with fear and pain
By wickedness the world will know
I am the way that men will go.

Kill the child and to be sure,
kill all the children born before
and all those that are not yet two,
put hurt and hate in what you do,
so that when you kill the special one
my wealth and safety will be won.

Archangel O obstinate children of a beloved God
Gabriel   Come now awake,
Your Lord is given unto you
He who stretched the heavens – spread the earth,
His son has come by Holy birth.

Herod	But I am the Lord of earth,
	the conqueror of men,
	the master of wills.
	By affluence and ease,
	my style, my way, my expertise
	I allow to those in my control
	a shallow life, I own their soul.
	They need life's little pleasures,
	they hate and fight, amass their treasures
	but I, the King, hold back their minds –
	to serve me well and preserve the times.

Archangel Michael	O you lordly Satan Herod
	what power you wield –
	but men don't know it.
	They do not strive to find a way
	you provide their wants for their decay.
	Since Adam left that Eden garden
	how could he seek a Godly pardon
	with you, at every step behind him,
	turning his mind to easily follow
	you, in every squalid hollow.
	But now a Saviour has been given.
	Our God has come to us from heaven.

Herod	But I want the earth
	To own mankind
	I'll fight this child: erase his birth,
	Lay traps for men to steal their minds.

Michael	So by the power of heaven
	I confuse your plans.
	The child, you never will discover.
	Power is given from above
	and comes to man to show God's love,
	I drive you out – do not return
	leave man alone —— in Hades burn.

The Flight Into Egypt

(A Continuation from the Script of the Wintershall Nativity Play)

Michael   And so this revered, beloved babe,
by Gabriel led to Egypt rides,
until the fears of Herod fade
and then, with Joseph by their side,
Sweet Mary and the Jesus boy
at home in Cana will abide.

This greatest birth, this sign for man,
this beginning breath by God, as man on earth,
this tiny babe rings out a chime
to peal the ages deep in time.
We are no longer stained and stranded
on this distant rim of land
– we have a sign for those who grasp it,
We have a lead
for those who take it,
Come see the light,
come praise the birth,
God's son has descended to our earth.

Lord Williams of Shamley Green

So old Leo's dead –
shaved, dressed and ready,
he fell dead in his own kitchen,
whilst his wife slumbered.
He had smoked so hard to hide.

He was of the hunter and warrior class,
Brave in action – in war – in the
front row – in all the outside –
His living was gracious, his laughter strong, his smile always.
In another life almost a god
but not in ours.
This time around Leo, my friend, smoked,
to hide from the world he could not handle.